GUIDE
DOGS

from puppies to partners

Diana Lawrenson

ALLEN & UNWIN

In memory of my mother, June,
who transcribed many books into Braille

and remembering Felix

Members of the International Federation of Guide Dog Schools for the Blind have major similarities, minor differences, and meet specified standards in the training of guide dogs and subsequent instruction of vision impaired people. Each school has a common aim: to provide vision impaired people with independence through the use of a guide dog. The Guide Dog Association of Victoria, Australia, whose practices and premises this book largely reflects, is a member.

I am extremely grateful to the Guide Dog Association of Victoria for granting me access to their facilities and staff, and to both John Gosling and Kay Nattrass for their support and information. My sincere thanks go to Loretta Walshe who arranged interviews, organised photographs, and shared her knowledge with enthusiasm, and to the people who generously told me about their work, their lives and their dogs: Melinda Bito, Melissa Charles, Jane Dunham, Sonya Farlech, Mark Fisher, Russell Frank, Anton Hackenberger, Darryl Haley, the Harvey family, Diana Hatchley, Peter McNabb, David Markham, Donna Murdoch and Edwina Rea. To Rosalind Price, Sue Flockhart and Sandra Nobes who contributed to this book in various ways – thank you.

I appreciate very much the kindness of the following photographers in giving permission to reproduce their works, knowing a portion of the proceeds from this book is supporting the work of the Guide Dog Association of Victoria:
©Rob Anderson, Phoenix Studio page 3, page 31 (bottom)
©Graham Baring page 4
©Andrew Brownbill, Leader Newspaper Group page 7 (top)
©Kate Garretty page 24
©Lucy Morton pages 7 (bottom), 8, 9, 25 (bottom left)
©Michael Silver pages 1, 5, 6, 10, 11, 12, 13. 14, 15 (bottom), 16, 17 (three on right), 18, 19, 20, 21, 23, 25 (three on right), 26, 27, 28, 29, 30, 31 (top)
©Jay Town, The Herald & Weekly Times Photographic Collection page 15 (top)

Staff from the Guide Dog Association of Victoria, handlers and holders who feature in this book are: Merle Atherton, Katherine Atkinson, Jun Atobe, Melinda Bito, Paula Foote, Sue Hawkins, Candice Hilton, Justin Marshall, Liz McColl, Lisa Price, Edwina Rea, Sally Robinson, Joan Smith, Peter Tomlins, Percy Wilson.
The dogs that feature in this book are: Britta, Floyd, Freddy, Helga, Lonnie, Lucy, Lundy, Melvin, Otus, Pedro, Quilton, Spike, Zadek and Zenith.

Contents

TOP DOGS

Guide dogs are top dogs. When they're in harness and working they are lifelines. Out of harness they are as playful as any pet.

Some people who use guide dogs are not totally blind, and not all blind people use guide dogs. Some people don't like dogs. Some are too old or too young. And some have additional disabilities that prevent them using a dog.

A person who wants a guide dog must have:

- A vision impairment severe enough for the dog to be of real benefit to them
- A desire to use the dog as a working dog
- A sense of orientation – the ability to find their way about
- Sufficient hearing or vision to recognise traffic and the direction it's coming from
- Adequate balance
- The confidence and physical fitness to manage the dog
- A welcoming home – because a dog won't work well if it lives in a tense or unhappy place

Guide dog Jizbar with his handler and her pram tow. The pram is clipped to a belt around the mother's waist.

Labrador-retrievers, generally known as labradors, are the breed used most often as guide dogs, followed by golden retrievers, golden retriever-labrador crosses and German shepherds. But any dog that is fit and healthy, has a calm temperament and is willing to please may be suitable. Standard poodles, giant schnauzers, labradoodles and various working dogs, such as sheepdogs, are all guiding people in different parts of the world. Even boxers and a greyhound-labrador cross have guided.

'A powerful bond exists between a person and their dog,' says one Guide Dog Services manager. 'The dog enriches a person's life.'

There are more than seventy guide dog schools around the world. They work in similar ways, with some variations. For instance, they don't all breed their own puppies, and they begin training dogs at different ages. Some schools prefer guide dog handlers to be between 18 and 65, while others provide dogs for 16 year olds and have no upper age limit.

Yet every guide dog training school has a common goal: to provide a vision impaired person with independence through the use of a trained guide dog, free.

Many guide dog schools help each other. They might train staff for schools in other countries or send dogs to schools starting breeding programmes. Others exchange breeding dogs, or dogs' semen, to avoid in-breeding and the inheritance of weaknesses through related dogs. The results of research into guide dogs and their work is freely exchanged between member schools of the International Federation of Guide Dog Schools for the Blind.

DID YOU KNOW?
The first school for training guide dogs was established in Germany after many soldiers returned blind from World War 1.

DID YOU KNOW?
A young blind woman is a television newsreader in Spain. She finds Braille slow to read by touch, so she memorises most of it beforehand and speaks to the camera.

TOP: *Guide dog Druscilla is a labradoodle: a labrador-poodle cross*

CENTRE: *Labrador and German shepherd pups*

BOTTOM: *Guide dog instructor cadet*

BREEDING

A COLONY OF DOGS

A Guide Dog Centre's breeding colony of brood bitches and stud dogs live with families who are called breeding stock holders. All the breeding dogs have the temperament and physical qualities to make excellent guide dogs. 'They're the best of the best,' says a breeding manager who wants puppies to inherit the good qualities of their parents.

Stud dog Otus with his holder

A stud dog comes in to the breeding centre when he is needed for mating. A bitch boards at the breeding centre when she is in season, around every six months, and when it is time to give birth.

WHELPING

The time from conception to birth is approximately sixty-three days for puppies. Pregnant bitches come in to the breeding centre about ten days before their puppies are due, so if the pups arrive early they'll still be born in clinically clean surroundings with people immediately on hand to help if they need it.

Five days before the birth, called whelping, the bitch spends most of her time in a whelping room to become used to it. Her temperature is taken twice a day and when it drops the staff know whelping will start in about twenty-four hours.

She begins to nest when labour starts, burrowing into the bedding and tearing up blankets in the whelping box until she delivers the first pup. Day or night, staff watch on closed circuit television in a viewing room, usually without disturbing her. 'We watch to make sure she breaks the sac, clears the puppy's nostrils and mouth by licking, and that the puppy's alive,' says the breeding manager. 'If we have any doubts we might go in and help her, particularly a maiden bitch – a first-time mother. But generally we let nature take its course, which is best for the bitch and best for the puppies.'

A student with brood bitch Lucy, whose holder is a teacher

Sometimes staff do need to break the sac and massage the pup's body with a towel to make it breathe. If it doesn't respond they'll start cardiopulmonary resuscitation, using the side of a thumb on the pup's tiny rib cage and blowing down its nose. But often the only human touch is a spot of colour painted on each puppy's head to mark the order of its birth, and to indicate which pup is which for weighing.

Each bitch has a separate whelping room because some are very protective of their puppies. Staff can look in through darkened one-way glass but the bitch can't see them.

The breeding centre is kept very clean because an outbreak of disease could kill a lot of puppies. Staff dip the soles of their shoes in disinfectant footbaths before entering, and the rooms are scrubbed every day.

Lucy and her litter in the whelping box

PUPPIES

WEEK 1

At birth most labrador puppies weigh between 340 and 440 grams, and are about as long as an adult's hand. They can't open their eyes or hear, they mew like kittens, and they wriggle because they can't walk yet. They are totally dependent, suckling from their mother frequently, day and night, and sleeping beside her in the whelping box.

Animal nurses check the puppies many times each day and take the bitch outside to stretch and relieve herself. Bedding is changed daily, or more often if it's dirty. It's washed and dried in the breeding centre's laundry.

Every second day each puppy's weight gain is recorded.

WEEK 2

The puppies' eyes start to open and they begin responding to sounds. They are growing fast and are now weighed only once a week.

The bitch waits at the door when she wants to go outside, and staff take her for a daily walk.

The bitch, her pups and the whelping box are moved from their whelping room to their own day room with a sheltered outdoor area for the pups

to play in when they're a bit bigger. They still snuggle together in the whelping box, keeping close to their mother for food and warmth.

The puppies begin medicines to keep them free from worms.

WEEK 3

The puppies start walking but they're wobbly and tire quickly. Staff pick them up and stroke them a lot so they get used to people. It's the beginning of the trust and bond between animal and human that's so important for their future. 'The more pups are handled the better they'll be in later life,' says an animal nurse.

The puppies' teeth start coming through and weaning begins. Soft canned meat is introduced to the pups three times a day. Now they drink less milk from the mother and she is taken outside while they eat. 'Otherwise she'd scoff their food,' says the breeding manager.

The whelping box is removed because the puppies are walking and not so dependent on their mother for food. They sleep on sheet-covered blankets.

Newborn puppies

OPPOSITE: *Lucy's multi-coloured litter*

8

Puppies starting dried food

WEEK 4

The puppies begin dried food with the puppy meat and start drinking water. The bitch makes less milk because the puppies are not feeding from her so much.

Staff give the puppies lots of attention. 'This is my favourite stage of the puppies' development,' says an animal nurse. 'They are developing their own personalities and temperaments.'

Volunteers caress and play with the puppies in the playground to help the animal nurses socialise them at this important time. The puppies have their own miniature adventure park with ramps and tunnels and space for them to explore and tumble about.

WEEK 5

The mother spends her day in an enclosure with other bitches, except for her daily walk and lunchtime when she's brought back to feed her puppies. This is the last week the puppies sleep with her at night.

Each puppy now has its own bowl and is fed the correct amount of food for its size and weight. They play in their day room and in its outdoor area. 'If we see a puppy roughing up its brothers and sisters we correct it with a low, gruff *No!* – like a grumbly bark its mother would give if she was there,' says the breeding manager.

A number is tattooed on each puppy's ear and a tiny microchip is injected under the loose skin between the shoulders to identify the pup as a member of the guide dog community for its life.

Each year the litters are listed in alphabetical order: A litter, B litter, up to Z, and every puppy has a name beginning with its litter's letter.

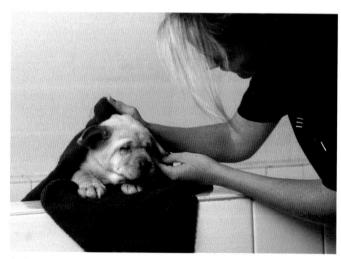

Bath time

There are names like Jazz, Drewfus, Skeeter and Heartly, or familiar ones like Amy and Alex, but no working guide dogs from the centre have the same name. Occasionally competitions are held to find more, and staff keep dozens of name books. The letters U, X and Y might be skipped unless there are only one or two puppies in the litter.

WEEKS 6 TO 7

By now the pups are fully weaned. The animal nurses take them out to explore and scuffle on the grass. They have soft toys to play with and are given rawhide strips to chew. The pups are gently introduced to wearing a collar and walking on a leash.

They have the first of their vaccinations to protect them against the life-threatening diseases parvovirus, distemper and hepatitis. Kennel cough vaccination is given later.

It's time for each puppy to go and live with a puppy raiser for their first year.

WEEKS 7 TO 8

The animal nurses check the bitch's milk has dried up and that she doesn't have mastitis – an infection of the mammary glands where she made her milk. She goes home again to her holder until her next season.

Staff become attached to the 'broodies', their name for the breeding bitches, because they stay at the breeding centre for about three months every year. On average each bitch has a litter once every eighteen months. 'They all have their own personality,' says an animal nurse. 'Some are very affectionate and smoochy, some are placid, and others are cheeky and playful. One of our older ones, Kath, always has a smile.'

LEFT: *Weigh day*

RIGHT: *Lots of loving contact from an early age*

11

PUPPY RAISING

Puppies grow out of collars and coats faster than you grow out of clothes. 'Raising a puppy is like watching someone grow up, except it all happens in one year,' says a puppy raiser.

Puppy raisers must not leave their puppy alone for more than three hours a day. The pup spends a lot of time indoors with people because as a guide dog it will live beside someone day and night. If the puppy raiser has a family, the pup respects an adult as the pack leader and sees the children as its equals, even though they may help feed and groom it.

A puppy raising supervisor visits every four to six weeks to give advice and support. House training starts the day the puppy arrives.

Gradually it learns to relieve itself outside on the command 'Quick, quicks!', which is important for its future work.

While the puppy is small, the puppy raiser often carries it when they go out, and always speaks to the pup in a reassuring voice. Over a year the puppy raiser and the supervisor will help it get used to people and noise. They want the pups to be relaxed going to shops, or football matches, and even when walking past dogs and cats in the street.

The puppy raiser uses deeper voice tones to reprimand the puppy, and rewards it with praise and pats for doing something correctly. 'It's important pups learn to listen to a quiet voice for all their commands so they respond calmly and don't become anxious,' says a supervisor.

Going for a walk with the puppy raiser and supervisor

Puppy Freddy and guide dog Melvin with their puppy raiser and Melvin's handler

Zadek waiting quietly while the puppy raiser drinks coffee

Walking in a busy street

The puppy is taught basic terms such as 'Sit' and 'Stay'. It learns to walk on a leash; to sit and wait for the command to eat when its food is put down; and not to jump on beds and furniture. 'We don't want dogs grabbing food, or barging through a doorway first, or jumping up on people,' says a supervisor. Once a pup leapt into a bath a puppy raiser's daughter had run for herself. It had to hop out because a puppy raiser must insist on obedience to remain the pack leader.

Puppies can board at the Guide Dog Centre's kennels when the family goes on holidays or if the puppy raiser is ill. When the young dog is about twelve months old the puppy raiser returns it to the centre. Parting is always hard.

Five months later the puppy raiser attends the dog's graduation and watches it guiding a trainer. They say goodbye again. 'It's sad, but a happy sadness,' the puppy raiser says. 'We know there's someone waiting for the dog.'

Freddy learning to sit for his meal

LIVING AT THE

Animal nurse preparing individual meals in the kennel kitchen

Meals are prepared in the kennels' kitchen. The amount of food for each dog, depending on its weight, is written beside its name on a whiteboard. Named bowls are filled with exact quantities of tinned meat and dried food, and loaded on to a trolley. As it rattles along the chorus of barks is deafening, but each dog must sit quietly before its bowl is put down.

An animal nurse grooms the dog every second day in the treatment room. As she brushes its coat she checks the dog all over, from inside its ears to the pads of its paws. She writes health comments on the dog's record card and gives any medicine the vet has ordered. Each dog is shampooed at least every three weeks.

The vet visits the kennels' clinic once a week to diagnose and treat any puppies or dogs that are unwell, and to give vaccinations. Specialists from the university veterinary school take x-rays

When a young dog moves in to the kennels the animal nurse gives it a shampoo and flea rinse. The dog is coaxed to climb steps to a raised shower in the kennel bathroom, to help it become used to steps anywhere.

Two dogs share a kennel, but it's not an ordinary dog kennel. It's a small room with a window, an infra-red lamp for warmth at night, and under-floor heating for winter. On the door is a board with each dog's name, colour, sex, tattoo and yard number.

In the morning the dog's trainer lets it out into its yard. Staff mix the dogs so that the group of four in each yard get along and don't fight. 'We want them all to be relaxed here,' says an animal nurse. Every yard has a shelter. On hot days the dogs enjoy playing under water showering from hoses and once a day they go for a romp on a grass run.

Putting drops in a dog's ear

KENNELS

and perform any necessary operations. Afterwards the dogs recover in the air-conditioned clinic kennels where the nurses pamper them with extra attention and toys.

Every day the kennels, treatment rooms, bathrooms and yards are scrubbed with disinfectant and hosed down.

One resident at the Guide Dog Association of Victoria kennels is not a dog. Tim the cat wanders wherever he likes. 'He prefers dog food to cat food, lazes around all day and scratches the dogs if they come too close,' says an animal nurse. Trainers can easily see which dogs want to chase Tim...

ASSESSMENT: THE
BIG TEST

'It's a big change to leave a loving home and move in to kennels with a group of dogs your own age,' says a guide dog trainer.

After a few days settling in, each dog is taken on a series of five walks to assess whether its temperament is calm and willing enough to train as a guide dog. The walks progress from a quiet area on the first day to a busy street of shops with public transport rumbling past on the fifth day.

The trainer tests and notes the dog's reactions. Does it respond well to commands? Is it frightened by sudden loud noises? Is it distracted by a cat or another dog? Fifteen temperament traits are scored, and a dog

DOG TEMPERAMENT & HEALTH ASSESSMENT

Dog ID:_____   Dog Name:_____

Sire: _____   Dam: _____

TEMPERAMENTAL TRAIT:	V.GOOD	GOOD	SATISFACTORY	POOR	V.POOR	SCORE
Suitable Willingness	A+ A A-	B+ B B-	C+ C C-	D+ D D-	E+ E E-	_____
Suitable Concentration	A+ A A-	B+ B B-	C+ C C-	D+ D D-	E+ E E-	_____
Suitable Body Sensitivity	A+ A A-	B+ B B-	C+ C C-	D+ D D-	E+ E E-	_____
Suit Voice Responsiveness	A+ A A-	B+ B B-	C+ C C-	D+ D D-	E+ E E-	_____
Lack of Suspicion	A+ A A-	B+ B B-	C+ C C-	D+ D D-	E+ E E-	_____
Lack of Anxiety	A+ A A-	B+ B B-	C+ C C-	D+ D D-	E+ E E-	_____
Lack of Excitability	A+ A A-	B+ B B-	C+ C C-	D+ D D-	E+ E E-	_____
Lack of Dog Distraction	A+ A A-	B+ B B-	C+ C C-	D+ D D-	E+ E E-	_____
Lack of Cat Distraction	A+ A A-	B+ B B-	C+ C C-	D+ D D-	E+ E E-	_____
Lack of Food Distraction	A+ A A-	B+ B B-	C+ C C-	D+ D D-	E+ E E-	_____
Lack of Scent Distraction	A+ A A-	B+ B B-	C+ C C-	D+ D D-	E+ E E-	_____
Lack of Aggression	A+ A A-	B+ B B-	C+ C C-	D+ D D-	E+ E E-	_____
Lack of Fear	A+ A A-	B+ B B-	C+ C C-	D+ D D-	E+ E E-	_____
Lack of Sound Shyness	A+ A A-	B+ B B-	C+ C C-	D+ D D-	E+ E E-	_____
Acceptable Dominance	A+ A A-	B+ B B-	C+ C C-	D+ D D-	E+ E E-	_____

Lowest & Overall Score   _____

Acceptable Health: Skeleton   Yes / No   Physiology   Yes / No   Skin Yes / No

Recommended Outcome:

Breeding ☐   GD Trng ☐   Reassess ☐   Reboard ☐   Reclassify ☐

Chart showing temperament traits the trainer assesses

must receive 'very good' or 'good' in *every* aspect to begin training. If it scores 'satisfactory' in one or more categories, the dog is taken on extra walks for a month to increase its confidence. Then it will be assessed again. But any dog that scores 'poor' or 'very poor' for even one trait will not pass.

The dog's health must be first-class, too. Bones, joints, skin, hearing and nervous system are all checked. A vet who specialises in animal ophthalmology examines the dog's eyes to ensure they are perfect, because a guide dog sees for its handler.

Testing the dog's reaction to sudden loud noises (sound shyness) with a starter's gun

TRAINING

THE VAN

It takes a walk a day, five days a week, for five months to train a guide dog. Trainers take out three dogs at a time in a van, and they always park in the shade or under cover. In the van are:

- bottles of water and bowls
- leashes and correction collars
- a full harness and a harness without the handle
- towels to dry the dogs on wet days
- a blindfold for the trainer to wear when the dog is near the end of its training
- bags to collect dog droppings

THE DAILY WORKOUT

The trainer works with one dog for about forty-five minutes while the others wait in the van. Waiting patiently is part of a guide dog's work.

On hot days the dogs train early in the morning before pavements are too hot for their paws. As they learn more they practise every-thing in different places: residential streets, suburban shopping areas and the city. A dog's body language shows how well it's coping. If it's ears are relaxed and the tail is out, or gently wagging, the dog is alert and comfortable. But flattened, pulled-back ears and a tail that's down mean the dog is worried.

Although trainee and qualified guide dogs all wear correction collars, they are not used very often. 'Generally you can train a dog by talking to it, using praise,' says a trainer. Lots of praise and pats, but never food, are the rewards for good work.

TOP: *Assessing for confidence on open steps*

CENTRE: *Training in a shopping centre*

BOTTOM: *Assessing for dog distraction*

LEARNING ON A LEASH

For the first weeks the trainer walks the dog with only a leash, in peaceful streets. The dog learns to obey basic obedience terms such as 'Heel', 'Sit' and 'Stay', and the trainer praises it when it responds to a command that is said only once, quietly. The dog becomes familiar with passing traffic, stopping at kerbs and crossing roads in response to a command. The trainer teaches it to walk in a straight line, and to lead a little ahead on the left side. As they walk around streets the trainer begins teaching the foot positions and hand signals for the dog to move right or left, or ahead on the command 'Forward'. The dog learns to return to walking in a straight line if they've had to go around obstacles, such as shrubbery overhanging a fence.

When there are distractions like food or people or animals passing, the trainer instructs 'No' or 'Leave' to stop the dog sniffing or showing interest.

DID YOU KNOW?

Some schools in Japan train dogs to walk on either the right or the left side so that the dog is always between the person and any open stormwater drains.

TOP: *Learning to walk past a distraction*

CENTRE/BOTTOM: *Learning to guide around an obstruction. Note the trainer's hand signals for 'Stay' in centre picture and then 'Find the way' below.*

Learning to walk calmly as a skateboarder whizzes past

OPPOSITE: *Helga, in a body piece only, with her trainer*

Gradually the dog is introduced to busier areas. They go into shops, just as the dog did with its puppy raiser. The trainer might introduce terms such as 'Find the shop' or 'Find the counter' without expecting a response, simply to familiarise the dog with commands its handler will use in the future.

THE HARNESS

In the second month a body piece – the leather harness without the handle – is fitted. 'We start with an old one because it's comfortable for a dog to wear the first time,' says a trainer. 'Most dogs accept it. They might look around at it a few times, but most adapt to it.' On rare occasions a dog doesn't. So for a few days the dog is given its meal while the body piece is put on, and soon it wears the leather accessory contentedly. The harness handle is attached two to four weeks later, and training proceeds with the dog wearing the full harness, leash and correction collar: its complete working outfit.

TRAVELLING OUTDOORS AND IN

The trainer helps the dog get used to climbing both solid and open stairs, and become familiar with all sorts of public transport. Eventually the dog will learn the correct way to enter and alight from buses, trams and trains. On board it's taught to lie with its haunches beneath the seat so it's not thrown off balance when the vehicle moves off or turns corners. On railway platforms a dog learns to stand back from the edge.

They go to indoor shopping centres and the city many times, at first to become used to crowds and noise, and later to walk through department stores and learn how to travel on escalators and travelators and in lifts.

Gradually the dog begins to initiate action, for instance stopping at a kerb without being told, and waiting to hear the command 'Forward' before proceeding.

Learning to board a tram

AVOIDING OBSTACLES

One of the dog's hardest lessons is learning to allow enough space for both itself and its handler to walk *together*. 'Height is the most difficult thing to teach,' a trainer says. The dog must learn to guide a person around something at human head level, such as a branch, so that they don't hit their head.

The dog must learn about width to know whether there is enough room for it and a person to walk through narrow areas, like a pavement that is partially blocked with tables and chairs outside a restaurant or cafe. 'It's like someone riding a motorcycle,' says the trainer. 'They can weave through lines of cars because they're only looking after themselves and the bike. But if a sidecar is attached the rider has to allow for the extra width.'

Footpath obstructions, such as a car across a driveway, or excavations, are hazards for a vision impaired person and the dog learns how to guide around them, perhaps by moving on to the road to walk past.

Trainer showing the dog a bush to teach it to guide around it

Learning to wait calmly at a level crossing as a train passes

CROSSING ROADS

Dogs can see some colour, but we don't know exactly how much. We do know that dogs can't distinguish between red and green traffic lights.

In shopping strips where there are pedestrian crossings with traffic lights, the dog is taught 'Find the crossing'. It learns to stand close to the pole so the trainer can press the button. Even at a crossing with audible traffic signals the dog is supposed to wait for the instruction 'Forward' when the speed of the clicking changes. Some dogs gradually connect the word with the clicking speed, and might start to go, but the person in charge of the dog always listens to the traffic and corrects the dog if necessary.

The dogs also learn when *not* to cross roads. Two trainers work together, one with the dog and the other driving a car. At first the car is driven slowly, stopping at the kerb directly in front of the dog, and the trainer instructs the dog 'Forward'. The dog can't obey because the car is in the way, so the trainer praises it for not moving. Little by little, the car is driven from further away towards the dog on the kerb. Eventually the dog begins to understand that when it sees a vehicle coming it must not step off the kerb, even if it is told to move forward. Sometimes this is called 'intelligent disobedience'.

If a car drives through red lights or unexpectedly turns a corner when the dog is already on the road, the dog is trained to stop instantly – a lifesaving action.

DID YOU KNOW?

On a crowded vehicle a vision impaired person extends their foot beside the dog's to prevent passengers accidentally stepping on the dog's paw.

Assessing the dog's confidence on a railway platform

21

THE FIFTH MONTH

By now it's clear which dogs work well in busy or quiet areas, and which dogs are suited to reserved or outgoing people. Dogs and people are matched before the general training finishes, four weeks before they meet.

In the fifth month the dog revises everything. The trainer fine-tunes the training practice for the particular needs of the person the dog will guide. For instance, if that person is tall and travels to work by bus, they do additional height clearance work and bus trips. On occasions trainers wear blindfolds to ensure they are not inadvertently helping the dog.

The dog visits the centre's live-in residence to see and smell the home where it will stay temporarily with the person it is to guide. As a test, the trainer might eat in the dining room while the dog lies quietly under the table, and the smoke alarm will be set off. The dog should stay calm.

After twenty weeks the dog has learned to respond confidently to around thirty commands by word, hand or foot, at times refusing to obey for safety reasons. At last it will meet the person with whom it will bond as both a qualified guide dog and companion for the next eight to ten years.

DID YOU KNOW?

The Guide Dog Association of Victoria, Australia, provided a woman of 82 with her first guide dog, and years later they are still working well together.

COMMANDS

V=Voice, H=Hand signal, L=Leash, F=Foot position

Sit V L if necessary using the hands to correctly sit the dog

Stop V L F to stop and stand, usually when working in a harness

Down V H L

Wait V H to wait for a short period of time

Stay V H to stay in sit or down position for a more lengthy period of time

Forward V H F to set off on walk, or leave the kerb when crossing a road, always in harness

Back V H F to turn back and retrace steps, in harness

Left or Right V H F to turn 90 degrees left or right

Find left or right V H F to indicate a slight change of direction

Steady V to encourage dog to reduce its speed of walking

No V to discourage undesirable behaviour or a distraction

Leave it V as for 'No', specifically when confronted by a distraction such as other dogs or cats

Straight on V to encourage dog to move on smoothly ahead, especially if there is a hesitation

Find the way V when the situation is busy, like a shopping centre, and dog needs to find gaps and receive encouragement

Hup-hup V H F if dog cannot leave the kerb on Forward command due to traffic, then this encourages dog to proceed when it's clear

When you can V F as for 'Hup-hup'

Follow V to follow a sighted person, for example, to follow a shop assistant to go to a different department in the store

Okay V all clear, for example, to commence eating food presented in a bowl

Find the V F to cue a dog to a specific destination, for example, a door, bank, seat

Good boy/girl V reward for doing well

That's better V reward for improving performance, for example, after there has been a distraction

BEGINNING TOGETHER

Imagine waiting to meet your dog. You're sitting on the floor or a chair so you're at the dog's level because standing over it is a dominant position. Will you like each other? Will you mind sharing almost every moment with it? Will you trust the dog with your life?

'From the beginning I absolutely adored Lundy, but to actually trust her to get me across roads and take me around, well, that's putting a lot in a dog's hands,' says Melissa Charles. 'Now I totally trust her.' It takes time to establish trust.

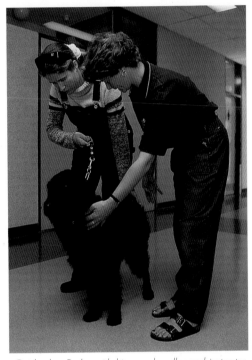

Guide dog Pedro with his new handler and instructor

People live in at a Guide Dog Centre for four weeks to learn how to handle a guide dog. First an instructor teaches hand signals and foot positions on practise walks, using an empty harness because learning on a dog would confuse it. Then there's leash control. Everyone learns how to feed, groom, wash and clean up after their dog, how to walk around the streets with the dog in harness, and how to use public transport together. Gradually each person bonds with their dog and becomes its new pack leader.

At home the instructor helps the dog settle in with other family members and any pets. The dog can relax out of harness. The instructor goes through the person's travel and transport routes for work and shopping with the dog, teaching particular commands the person needs, such as 'Find the post office'.

The dog and the vision impaired person become a close team. The dog provides its new handler with smoother mobility and increased independence, and the handler provides the guide dog with leadership and loving care.

DID YOU KNOW?

A cabinet minister has a guide dog that accompanies him into the House of Commons in the British Parliament.

TOP: *Candice meeting her dog, Pedro, at the centre's residence*

CENTRE: *Instructor teaching hand signals on an empty harness*

BOTTOM: *Grooming Pedro*

TEAMS OF TWO
RUSSELL FRANK and SPIKE

Russell and his working dogs

Russell Frank lives and works on a farm with his guide dog, Spike. Sometimes Spike guides Russell to the stock saleyards in the local town or by train to meetings in the city.

'Having Spike is like having two dogs,' Russell says. 'Out of harness, at home, he tears around the paddocks – he's a ratbag. But as soon as the harness is on he's totally different.'

Spike adapted quickly to cattle and sheep, but hides behind Russell if the goats come near because they headbutt him. Russell shears sheep by using touch. Spike jumps into the holding pen and nudges a sheep up to the gate when Russell is ready to pull it on to the boards for shearing. In the paddocks Russell only has to say, 'Find the gate on the other side,' or 'To the water trough,' and Spike will take him there.

Russell has an artificial eye, but after an accident with a fishing rod he lost nearly all the sight in his good eye. He could no longer work as an operating theatre technician or drive a car. Now Spike guides Russell to classes where he's taking a farm management course and a degree in welfare practices. Russell uses a screen reader computer software programme that reads the text of books and emails aloud, and he touch-types for exams and to send emails.

DID YOU KNOW?

Many vision impaired people learn to orientate themselves with a white cane before they are matched with a guide dog.

TEAMS OF TWO
SONYA FARLECH and BRITTA

Sonya Farlech was a student nurse when within one week she lost most of her sight. 'I knew vision loss was possible because I have diabetes, but it was still a shock when it happened so suddenly,' she says. 'You take your vision for granted.'

Sonya decided to continue living in her cottage with her partner and her pet labrador, Jake, even though her parents wanted her to move back home. After twelve months indoors, she learned to use a white cane and started to go out on her own.

A year later she was matched with Britta. 'She's wonderful. She's made my life so much easier.' Sonya is now doing a three-year diploma in community services. In class Britta lies quietly beside her. A support person helps Sonya with research and any text handouts. Sonya records the lectures and at home keys her own notes from the recording on to her computer, reversing the screen contrast to have large white text on a black background, which she can read. The computer has a screen reader, but Sonya also listens to friends and family reading books she needs, and to books recorded specially for her studies.

The dogs, Jake and Britta, have become the best of friends, and Sonya says, 'Britta's made a *huge* difference to me. I've always got a companion wherever I am.'

DID YOU KNOW?
A guide dog and its handler walk an average of 1,000 kilometres a year together.

Sonya and Britta

TEAMS OF TWO
MELISSA CHARLES and LUNDY

Melissa Charles has ridden horses since she was three. But at 20, a serious riding accident left her in hospital with severe injuries. When she regained consciousness most of her sight had gone.

Three years later Melissa and Lundy were matched.

Lundy sleeps in Melissa's bedroom and also has a bed in the living area. Two days a week they work at an airport where Melissa is a receptionist for a helicopter service.

Melissa has diabetes. Three times a week she travels with Lundy to hospital for renal dialysis while she waits for a kidney and pancreas transplant. The nurses provide a bowl of water and a lambskin for Lundy to lie on beside Melissa's chair during treatment. Out of harness Lundy often makes friends with other patients who are also there for dialysis.

Melissa hopes to ride her horse, Crescent, in the paralympics. They do dressage through Riding for the Disabled. 'Even though I was an experienced rider before, I've learned so many new things,' Melissa says.

Melissa, Crescent and Lundy

Clicking metronomes on the boundaries tell her where she is on the arena.

Lundy calmly accepts Crescent, but Melissa ties her to a fence before she rides. 'I won't let her too close because I'm scared Crescent might stand on her and break her bones so she'd never be able to work again.' Lundy watches all the time and can't wait for Melissa to dismount. Melissa says it's as if Lundy's thinking 'What are you sitting on that big dog for? Why aren't you with me?'

TEAMS OF TWO
DARRYL HALEY and LONNIE

Lonnie, Darryl and his daughter

The motorist drove through a red light. 'I heard the brakes and the car sliding towards us,' says Darryl Haley. 'Immediately Lonnie turned away and by the time we'd gone around in a circle the car had passed. If I hadn't had Lonnie I'd have been hit.'

Lonnie is Darryl's third guide dog, and they travel to work by train. 'Same carriage, same seat every day,' Darryl says. At the end of the hour's journey Lonnie leads Darryl up the escalators from the underground station and through the peak hour traffic to work. Darryl is a switchboard operator on the seventh floor of a city building, and Lonnie selects any one of five lifts to take them up. Darryl's dogs have never missed the seventh floor once, even though each floor looks the same, and no matter how often the lift stops on the way.

At the office Darryl takes off the harness and Lonnie relaxes on a dog bed. 'At lunchtime I take him downstairs to do what dogs have to do. He has a bit of a roll, a stretch and a walk and then we come up again.'

Lonnie goes fishing with Darryl at a surf beach, at the river or from a pier. 'We can sit for a couple of hours and not catch anything,' Darryl says, although once Lonnie ate half a packet of whitebait while he waited. On holidays Lonnie has his own bed in the campervan. 'He's perfect. Absolutely perfect,' says Darryl.

DID YOU KNOW?

Guide dogs sometimes work out other protective actions themselves. One dog pushed against its handler's legs to prevent him getting into a swimming pool – when the man wanted to go for a swim! Three days later, after walking up and down the pool anxiously as the handler swam laps, the dog settled and just watched.

ONGOING SUPPORT

Any problems that a person and their dog might have are most likely to occur in their first year together, so the Guide Dog Centre gives them plenty of support. Maybe they have to pass several aggressive dogs behind fences each day, or perhaps there are distractions in the street the dog has never come across before. An instructor visits a team four times in their first twelve months, and once a year after that to check they are working well. But a handler can phone at any time for help. Their instructor will advise or visit them wherever they live, or occasionally bring the dog back to the centre for extra training.

If a person moves house, changes jobs or takes up a different leisure activity, the team is retrained for the new travel route.

After eight to ten years a dog's working life is over. Its hearing or sight may begin to fail, or it may become arthritic and not so eager to get into harness for another day's work. Instructors always check older dogs carefully for any signs of slowing down.

'I cried my eyes out when Zenith retired,' says Darryl Haley. 'I said I didn't want another dog. I thought there'd never be another dog as good, but there was.'

DID YOU KNOW?

In Japan there is a home for retired guide dogs where their former handlers can visit them whenever they like.

Some retired dogs go to other family members or friends, but most remain with the family while the handler starts again with a young dog. A few people revert to a cane until the old dog dies.

DID YOU KNOW?

A handler who has had a limb amputated or who has an injury can have a dog trained to walk on the right side instead of the left.

DIFFERENT CAREERS FOR DOGS

Only about half the young dogs pass the assessment to train as guide dogs. What happens to the ones that don't?

A few very active ones are tested for their ability to detect and if they are good sniffers they might work for a police bomb detection unit. Others are offered back to their puppy raisers, a few are sold to new owners as pets, and some become companion dogs for children or adults who have special needs, such as a long-term illness or an intellectual disability.

But what if a dog develops a problem *after* it starts training?

Maybe one temperament trait was borderline in the assessment. Perhaps the dog isn't showing enough confidence or initiative, as more is expected of it. Well, instead of wearing a harness and working as a guide dog, it may become a companion dog, or a pets-as-therapy dog.

'These reclassified dogs are placid and soft-natured,' says the pets-as-therapy coordinator. 'It's a chance for a young vision impaired person to become used to a dog long before they are matched with a guide dog.'

Floyd is a pets-as-therapy labrador who lives with the Harvey family and two students, Anton and Sally. They attend a school for the blind during the week and go home to their own families in the country at weekends. Floyd is sometimes boisterous, always loving, and not always perfect. He plays tug-o'-war with Anton after school, and they enjoy walking together in a park with Marg Harvey. Sally is getting used to Floyd's furry feel, and the Harvey girls help feed and look after him.

Floyd and Anton

LOOKING FOR FUNDS

Raising and training each dog costs thousands of dollars.

So much dog and puppy food is needed it's delivered to the Guide Dog Centre in a semitrailer. Other essentials are dog raincoats, collars, leashes, harnesses and medicines. And the skilled staff who breed, train and care for the dogs, instruct the vision impaired people, and run the administration all need to be paid.

Marketing departments promote guide dogs through television, radio and the press, to keep people aware of the cost of guide dog mobility. Support comes in various ways:

- Personal or group sponsorship of individual puppies and dogs
- Corporate sponsorship of big expenses, such as dog food, pharmaceutical supplies or advertisements, which may be provided free or at a substantial discount, sometimes in return for the Guide Dog Centre displaying a company's name or logo
- Free media publicity
- Donations and bequests
- Volunteers such as puppy socialisers and puppy raisers
- Community fundraisers. In France, ninety young people gave an orchestral benefit concert, and a French Guide Dog School sells a book on dog obedience through veterinary clinics.

In England, balls, gala weekends and dinner dances are held, while in Australia all sorts of goods are telemarketed.

Newsletters keep supporters up to date with dogs and the latest activities. Some centres hold Open Days when people can experience walking blindfolded with a cane through an obstacle course, or watch puppies playing and guide dogs working. 'It's our way of saying thank you to the public,' says a marketing manager. 'People *see* what we do.'

WHEN YOU SEE A GUIDE DOG...

A guide dog is on duty and working whenever its harness is on, even if it looks like it's snoozing under a restaurant table. In the street the handler is depending on it to be alert so there are no accidents. To help:

- Don't talk to a guide dog when it's working. It's concentrating.
- Never pat a guide dog in harness.
  Darryl Haley has a sign on Lonnie's harness that says, 'Please don't pet me, I'm working. Thank you!'
- Don't whistle at a guide dog.
  What if it looks at you instead of where it's guiding its handler?
- Never offer a guide dog any food.
  They're wonderful dogs that love to eat, and seeking or accepting any tit-bit is a potentially dangerous distraction. An overweight dog develops painful leg problems and may have to stop guiding early.
- Keep your own dog on a leash, *under control* and *away* from a guide dog. Guide dogs are trained to ignore all dogs while working, but if a guide dog is attacked or traumatised by another dog,

a vision impaired person will lose their independence until the dog recovers – and what if it doesn't?
A guide dog is too precious to lose.

DID YOU KNOW?

Scientists in the United States and Germany are developing a robot that they hope will eventually guide people.

GLOSSARY

Animal nurse a person who cares for puppies and dogs at the kennels

Bequest money left in a will to a person or organisation

Bitch a female dog

Body piece leather part of the harness that fits around a dog's body

Braille a system of raised dots that blind people feel to read. Developed by Louis Braille

Breeding colony a group of top quality male and female dogs used for breeding

Breeding centre a place where dogs are mated and puppies are born and cared for

Breeding manager the person responsible for the matching and mating of stud dogs and bitches to obtain puppies with the correct temperament and physical features for guiding, and responsible for the care of puppies at the breeding centre

Breeding stock holder the person/family with whom a stud dog or brood bitch lives

Brood bitch a female dog kept for breeding, the **dam**

Cane/long cane/white cane a long stick used by vision impaired people that helps them avoid objects and manage stairs

Client follow-up support for a vision impaired person after they go home with their dog

Correction collar a chain or leather collar connected to a leash and worn by a dog in harness. Used to correct a dog if necessary

Corporate sponsor a company that provides large donations and/or its products free or cheaply to an organisation

Foot positions directional command signals given by foot to a guide dog

Guide dog mobility walking in the community with the use of a guide dog

Hand signals directional command signals given by hand to a guide dog

Handler person in charge of a working guide dog

Harness leather strapping and a metal handle worn by a guide dog and which the vision impaired person holds as they walk together

Height clearance training teaching a dog how to guide its handler around objects above the ground that might strike a person in the face or on the head

Holder see **Breeding stock holder**

Instructor a person who works with a dog-and-person team, teaching the handler how to look after and direct their guide dog

International Federation of Guide Dog Schools for the Blind a group of more than 70 guide dog schools around the world whose members meet set standards on breeding, raising and training guide dogs and instructing the dogs' handlers

Intelligent disobedience a dog's refusal to obey a command in order to keep its handler safe

Litter puppies born from one pregnancy

Logo a company's design signature

Maiden bitch a brood bitch pregnant for the first time or with her first litter of pups

Manager, Guide Dog Services the person who oversees the breeding and training of dogs, and the instruction of guide dog handlers at a guide dog centre

Marketing and Communications manager the person responsible for coordinating community awareness of guide dogs and their

work and fundraising for the centre

Obstacle avoidance training teaching a dog how to guide a person around objects

Ophthalmology the study of the eye and its diseases

Pack leader the person whom the puppy/dog knows it must respect as its leader

Pets-as-therapy dog a dog that did not pass the training to become a guide dog and has been given to a vision impaired person as a pet

Puppy raiser a volunteer in the community who cares for a puppy for about a year

Puppy raising supervisor person from a guide dog centre who advises and supports a puppy raiser

Reclassified dogs dogs originally bred for guiding, but who don't graduate from training

Sac a membranous bag of fluid in which each puppy grows inside the bitch

Screen reader a computer programme that reads out text on the monitor

Season the time at which a bitch is able to conceive puppies

Semen sperm

Stud dog a male dog kept for breeding, the **sire**

Telemarket to sell goods by telephone

Trainer person who teaches a dog all it must do to become a guide dog

Vaccinations immunisations against infectious diseases

Vision/Visual impairment partial or total sight loss

Weaning transferring from a diet of the mother's milk to solid foods and water

Whelp to give birth

Whelping box open box in which a bitch gives birth, and in which she and the puppies stay for the next two to three weeks.

First published in 2001

Copyright © Diana Lawrenson, 2001

Allen & Unwin
83 Alexander Street
Crows Nest NSW 2065
Australia
Phone: (61 2) 8425 0100
Fax: (61 2) 9906 2218
Email: frontdesk@allen-unwin.com.au
Web: http://www.allenandunwin.com

National Library of Australia
Cataloguing-in-Publication entry:

Lawrenson, Diana.
Guide Dogs: from puppies to partners

ISBN 1 86508 247 3 (hb)
ISBN 1 86508 246 5 (pb)

1. Guide dogs. I. Title.

636.73

Cover photographs by Michael Silver and
Rob Anderson (front cover, bottom)
Designed by Sandra Nobes
Printed in China by Everbest Printing Co. Ltd.

1 3 5 7 9 10 8 6 4 2